Author:
Peter Cook has worked as a designer and art director in publishing for 30 years. He has written many articles for computer-industry magazines and newsletters, and created the electronic version of the **You Wouldn't Want to be** series for The Salariya Book Company website.

Artist:
Kevin Whelan has worked in advertising for over 14 years, he lives in Georgia.

Series creator:
David Salariya has illustrated a wide range of books and has created and designed many new series for publishers both in the UK and overseas. In 1989, he established The Salariya Book Company. He lives in Brighton with his wife, illustrator Shirley Willis, and their son Jonathan.

Editor:
Karen Smith

Consultant:
Carolyn Travers, The Plimoth Plantation Museum

Published in Great Britain in 2005 by
Book House, an imprint of
The Salariya Book Company Ltd
25 Marlborough Place, Brighton BN1 1UB

Please visit the Salariya Book Company at:
www.salariya.com

ISBN 0-531-123411 (Lib. Bdg.)
ISBN 0-531-12391-X (Pbk.)

Published in 2005 in the United States
by Franklin Watts
An imprint of Scholastic Library Publishing
90 Sherman Turnpike, Danbury, CT 06816

A CIP catalog record for this title is available from the Library of Congress.

Printed and bound in China.

Printed on paper from sustainable forests.

You Wouldn't Want to Sail on the Mayflower!

I'm looking forward to making a new home in America.

A Trip That Took Entirely Too Long

Written by
Peter Cook

Illustrated by
Kevin Whelan

Created and designed by
David Salariya

White Eagle LMC
1585 White Eagle Drive
Naperville, IL 60564

Franklin Watts®
A Division of Scholastic Inc.
NEW YORK • TORONTO • LONDON • AUCKLAND • SYDNEY
MEXICO CITY • NEW DELHI • HONG KONG
DANBURY, CONNECTICUT

Contents

Introduction

Your name is Priscilla Mullins and you are about to embark on one of the most famous journeys in American history — the voyage of the *Mayflower*. The year is 1620 and you are traveling with your parents and brother to escape religious persecution in England and to make a better life in the New World. Carrying 102 passengers — now known as Pilgrims — the *Mayflower* is headed for the colony of Virginia on the east coast of America. But the ship is blown off course and eventually lands on the coast of present-day Massachusetts, where a colony is established at Plymouth.

But this is in the future. First you must endure the hardships of the voyage: the cramped conditions, lack of privacy, poor food, and the winter storms of the Atlantic Ocean. It is a journey that will eventually leave you an orphan and there are many times when you wish that you had avoided sailing on the *Mayflower* — a trip that took entirely too long!

The Pilgrims

William (father)

Priscilla Mullins (you)

Robert Carter (servant)

Joseph (brother)

Alice (mother)

Your father was one of a small group of English Puritans that later became known as the Pilgrims. In the early 1600s a group of "Separatists" had broken away from the Church of England. They wanted to lead a simple life, based on the teachings of the Bible. In 1608 a group of Pilgrims led by William Brewster emigrated to Holland to escape religious persecution. They settled in Leiden, but were still unhappy with the restrictions on their civil rights. About half of the congregation voted to emigrate to America, deciding to settle in the colony of Virginia.

YOU WERE BORN in about 1602 in Dorking, a small village in the county of Surrey in southern England. Along with your family and a servant, you travel to the port of Southampton on the south coast of England. From there you will begin your voyage to the New World.

WILLIAM BREWSTER is the "ruling elder" of the Leiden Separatists and the Pilgrim's religious leader.

THE PILGRIM FATHERS is the name given to the colonists who will sail aboard the *Mayflower.*

THE LONDON VIRGINIA COMPANY holds the charter for Virginia and authorizes the Pilgrim's proposed new settlement.

Freedom of Worship

THE PEOPLE WHO JOINED the *Mayflower* were known as "Separatists" because they didn't follow the religious practices of the Church of England. They wanted a church where the minister and the congregation were more equal: where the clergy had no direct political power and where there was no need for clerical robes, altars and kneeling for prayers.

Bless our congregation, Lord.

Handy Hint

Don't become a Pilgrim, you could be persecuted for your beliefs!

ENGLISH ORIGINS. Most of the emigrants come from southern England. They will name their new homes for towns they left behind, such as Plymouth, Boston and Greenwich.

Areas shown are where Puritans emigrated from during the period of 1620-1675.

Main areas
Secondary
Other

Departure from Plymouth

THE *SPEEDWELL*
The Leiden group bought this ship to sail from Holland to England and then on to America. The *Speedwell* is only a third of the size of the *Mayflower*.

Your group joins the Pilgrims from Leiden in the port of Southampton. They had sailed earlier from Holland aboard the *Speedwell*. With your family and fellow Pilgrims you board the *Mayflower* and, on August 15th, 1620, the two ships set sail carrying 120 passengers between them. But the *Speedwell* begins to leak and has to make for port to be repaired. At Plymouth the leaders decided to abandon the *Speedwell* and move all of the passengers onto the *Mayflower*. Upset by the bad start and crowded conditions, a number of Pilgrims give up at this point. In all, the *Mayflower* holds 102 passengers when she finally departs from Plymouth on September 16th.

THE FIRST LEG. The map (right) shows the first leg of the journey, with the Leiden group sailing from Holland to Southampton. There they meet with other English Pilgrims before departing for America. But the leaking *Speedwell* forces the ships to stop for repairs at Dartmouth and Plymouth.

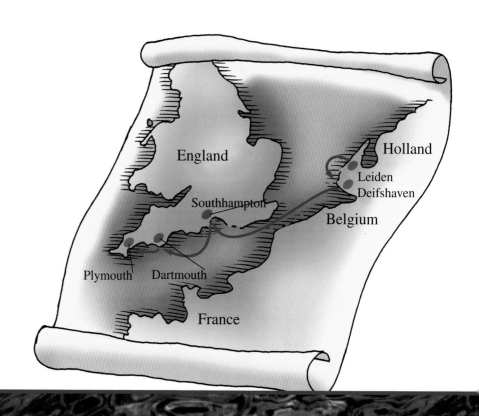

England

Holland

Leiden
Deifshaven

Southhampton

Belgium

Plymouth   Dartmouth

France

Loading the Mayflower

THE PILGRIMS have to take with them all of the clothes, tools, and equipment they would need in the New World — there are no shops there to buy new goods from. Your father is a boot and shoe maker and dealer and he loaded 250 shoes and 13 pairs of boots onto the *Mayflower*.

Handy Hint

Make sure your ship isn't leaking, or it could be a short trip!

This boot's got a hole in it!

The Mayflower

The 180-ton vessel is about 30 yard (27 meters), 9 yard (8 meters) wide and carries sails on three masts and a bowsprit. Along with the rest of the passengers you are berthed on the gun deck, which provides protection from the weather. It is a crowded space and you and your parents use simple dividers to make a small "cabin" to give you some privacy. You spend your time preparing food and helping your mother and other mothers with young children.

POOP HOUSE
Living quarters for the captain and some of the higher ranking crew.

CABINS
The sleeping quarters for the other crew members.

STEERAGE
Where the pilot steers the ship using a "whip-staff" — a stick that is moved back and forth to control the rudder.

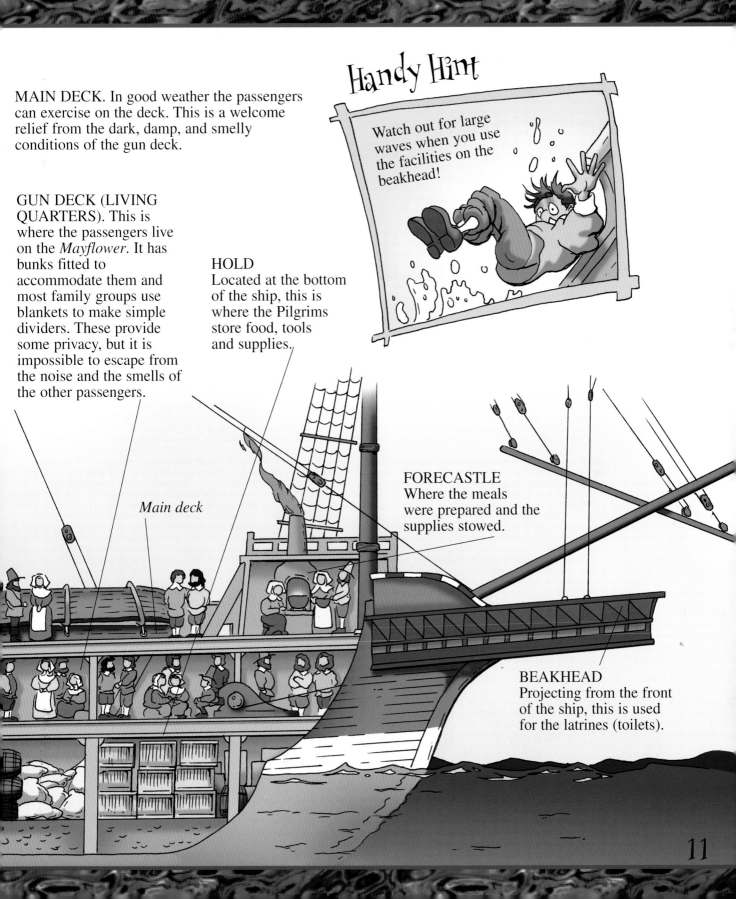

MAIN DECK. In good weather the passengers can exercise on the deck. This is a welcome relief from the dark, damp, and smelly conditions of the gun deck.

GUN DECK (LIVING QUARTERS). This is where the passengers live on the *Mayflower*. It has bunks fitted to accommodate them and most family groups use blankets to make simple dividers. These provide some privacy, but it is impossible to escape from the noise and the smells of the other passengers.

HOLD
Located at the bottom of the ship, this is where the Pilgrims store food, tools and supplies.

Handy Hint

Watch out for large waves when you use the facilities on the beakhead!

Main deck

FORECASTLE
Where the meals were prepared and the supplies stowed.

BEAKHEAD
Projecting from the front of the ship, this is used for the latrines (toilets).

The Crew

The *Mayflower* has a crew of about 30 (only a few of whom are now known by name). The ship's master (captain) is Christopher Jones, an experienced sailor about 50 years of age. He has a stake in the voyage, as he is part-owner of the *Mayflower*. The master's mates, John Clarke and Robert Coppin, have both sailed to Virginia and New England on earlier voyages. Giles Heale is the ship's surgeon and the 21-year-old John Alden is the ship's cooper (barrel maker). Young and handsome, Alden catches your eye early on in the voyage. Later he would decide to join the Pilgrims and eventually becomes your husband.

Important Crew Members

NAVIGATOR. He is responsible for plotting the ship's course.

HELMSMAN. He steers the *Mayflower* using the whipstaff.

SURGEON. He is responsible for the health of everyone on board.

Handy Hint

Make friends with the captain and crew, you may need their help later in the voyage!

The captain works us too hard. I might join the Pilgrims!

THE SAILMAKER maintains and repairs the ship's sails.

A GUNNER maintains and fires the ship's cannon if under attack.

COOPER. He makes and repairs barrels for storing water.

The Passengers

Who's Who:

WILLIAM BREWSTER is the Pilgrims' religious leader, responsible for approval from the London Virginia Company, who agreed to resettle them in America.

William Brewster

MILES STANDISH is a professional soldier, who was hired as a military advisor to the Pilgrims.

EDWARD WINSLOW will act as a diplomat, negotiating with the Native Americans and suppliers in England.

Miles Standish

Edward Winslow

William Bradford

WILLIAM BRADFORD will eventually become the governor of the Plimoth Colony, re-elected 30 times.

The 102 passengers live in close contact with one another for 66 days. They are formed from two groups (now known as the Leiden Contingent and the London Contingent). The 41 passengers from Leiden are led by William Brewster, Edward Winslow and William Bradford. Many of the men are adventurers, like Miles Standish, who is traveling to America to make his fortune rather than to escape religious persecution.

I can't wait to get to America!

Wives and children

EIGHTEEN OF THE MEN have brought their wives with them, while several left wives behind, concerned about the dangers and hardship involved in settling in a new colony. That proves to be a wise decision, for three-quarters of the women will die by the end of the harsh, first winter in the colony.

MANY FAMILIES brought their children with them, although several decided to leave them behind with relatives, planning to send for them once the colony is set up. There are 32 children and young people on board. Aged around 17, you are the eldest of the girls. All 11 girls survive the voyage and only two will die during the first winter.

Handy Hint

Get to know the other passengers, they could help if your family become ill or die!

15

Storms and Sickness

Many of the passengers suffer from seasickness, having never been at sea before. But by October, the *Mayflower* begins to encounter storms in the mid-Atlantic and life on board ship becomes increasingly miserable. You stay below deck most of the time, helping your mother to prepare food and trying to keep your clothes dry. Being on deck can be risky. During one storm a Pilgrim is swept overboard, but is saved by the crew.

ROCKED BY WAVES it is very difficult to cook and serve food. There is also the danger of fire spreading from the open ovens. In the worst weather everyone goes hungry.

SPRINGING LEAKS. The ship develops leaks, which the carpenter seals using oakum — hemp or jute fiber, treated with tar.

CRACKED BEAMS. A main beam cracks, but repairs are made using a large screw to hold the timber together.

SEASICKNESS. Most of the passengers suffer from seasickness. This weakens their resistance to other illnesses, such as pneumonia.

Handy Hint

Don't go on deck during a storm, you could be swept overboard!

Life and Death on the Mayflower

You've got no stomach for the sea, that's your problem!

hree of the women on board ship were pregnant when the voyage began. Elizabeth Hopkins gives birth to a son, whom she and her husband name Oceanus. Two other women are due to give birth shortly after the *Mayflower* reaches America. You get to know these mothers and help them in caring for their new babies. But the voyage also takes its toll. One of the sailors makes fun of the Pilgrims' discomfort and seasickness. He curses them daily, saying that he hopes to throw their dead bodies overboard and take their belongings for himself. But he is then among the first to die.

FIRST PILGRIM TO DIE. William Butten, one of the passengers, became ill and died three days before the *Mayflower* made landfall.

ONE OF THE SEAMEN taunted the sick Pilgrims. William Bradford wrote "it pleased God to smite this young man with a grievous disease, of which he died in a desperate manner and so was himself the first that was thrown overboard."

Land Ahoy!

The crew spot Cape Cod as the sun begins to rise on November 9th. The Atlantic storms had blown the *Mayflower* far north of her course to Virginia. At first the Pilgrim leaders decide to head south for the Hudson River (in present-day New York state).

But after encountering rough seas they agree to explore the Cape Cod region instead, anchoring in what is now Provincetown Harbor. Like everyone else on the ship, you are thrilled to finally see land and glad that your family has survived the dangerous voyage.

But the Pilgrim leaders have a dilemma. The land they have sighted is a long way from Virginia and they have had no rights granted to them to settle there.

LAND AT LAST. After 66 days at sea everyone is happy to see land again. But there is no one there to greet you. The land appears to be a wilderness, but Native Americans actually settled there many years earlier.

LAND AHOY! It's America!

Cape Cod Bay

Map labels:
- Provincetown
- Wellfleet
- (Patuxet)
- Plymouth
- Cape Cod Bay
- (Nobscusset)
- (Manomet)
- Sandwich
- (Cumaquid)
- Chatham

Handy Hint

Make sure your settlement is legal, otherwise it could be taken from you!

PEOPLE LIVE HERE! Although the land that the Pilgrims have sighted does not have any European settlers, there are a number of Indian tribes in the region. The map (left) shows the tribe names and the names of the towns that are eventually founded around Cape Cod Bay.

The Mayflower Compact

THE PILGRIM LEADERS know that the Cape Cod region is far north of the area in which The London Virginia Company granted them a right to settle. They decide to make their colony legitimate by signing the Mayflower Compact, which sets out the laws for their colony. It is signed on November 21st, 1620, by 41 of the *Mayflower*'s male passengers — including your father. Although today it is recognized as the first official document of American democracy, no women were allowed to sign it.

Exploring the Region

What happened when you landed?

In the first few days after landing the men explore the immediate region on foot. The Pilgrims had brought a small boat with them to explore the coastline, but it was damaged during the voyage. By the time it is repaired winter has set in and snow begins to fall. But on December 21st the boat enters the waters of what was to become known as Plymouth Harbor. At last a site has been found for the colony.

WASHING CLOTHES. You join the other women on the shore, where you wash clothes in a stream.

REPAIRING THE SHALLOP. The Pilgrims brought a 'shallop', a 30-foot single-sail boat, with them aboard the *Mayflower*. It had been dismantled for the voyage, but suffered some damage. It takes several weeks to repair the boat and make her seaworthy. During this time some of the men explore on foot. The women and children remain on board the *Mayflower* – there is no shelter on the shore.

EXPLORING THE COASTLINE
Once the shallop is repaired a party of men sets out to explore the coast. Over the course of several trips they follow the coastline around Cape Cod Bay, landing at different locations in search of a site for their colony. When they enter what is now known as Plymouth Harbor they find an ideal site, with fertile soil and fresh water.

Lookout for Indians!

THE EXPLORING PARTY is led by Captain Miles Standish, a professional soldier who was hired by the Pilgrims as military advisor. Armed with flintlock muskets, Standish and his men are ready to protect themselves if attacked. As they explore they see Indians at a distance, but only have one dangerous encounter: one night when they are camped on the shore a band of Indians fire arrows at them. No one is injured.

I hope the natives are friendly!

Handy Hint

Explore the region carefully. You don't want to build your colony in a swamp or some other poor location!

Building Plimoth Colony

Your New Home!

YOUR FIRST SIGHT of the new colony is a shock. There is nothing there except trees and wilderness. This is the first time you understand how hard it will be to build a new life in America. At times you regret ever leaving England.

The shallop returns to the *Mayflower* with news of a good site to establish a colony — this is named Plimoth (now Plymouth) after the port that you sailed from. The *Mayflower* sailed into the harbor and in the days that follow the men begin clearing the land and marking out the sites for their houses. Like most of the other women and children you remain on the *Mayflower*, waiting for the completion of the buildings. But you are kept busy, nursing the growing number of ill people.

But it's just a wilderness!

CLEARING THE LAND. The first task is to clear the land and mark out sites for houses and other buildings. It is agreed that the men will build their own homes, but they will co-operate to build a "common house" first. This is completed by mid-January, providing somewhere warm and dry to sleep.

BUILDING HOUSES. The trees cut down to clear the land are used to build simple wood-framed houses. Dry grass and sticks are gathered to thatch the roofs. In all seven houses and four store-houses are built, along with a "gun platform", which holds the cannon the Pilgrims brought, for defense from Indians and other enemies.

Handy Hint

Build your house as quickly as you can to avoid the worst of the winter weather!

Stop shirking!

NO HOLIDAYS. The men work in all weathers, even on Christmas Day. It is the end of March before everyone can move ashore. You can't wait because by now you have been living aboard the *Mayflower* for more than six months.

A Cruel Winter, then Thanksgiving

The "Great Sickness"

FIFTY of the Pilgrims — half your number — die during the first winter. All of your family are among those who perish.

While the men work on the land, illness spreads among the women on the *Mayflower*. By the time that the houses are ready, 13 of the original 18 have died. You nurse your father, mother and younger brother, but all of them die, leaving you an orphan. The crew sail the *Mayflower* back to England in April 1621, but the fortunes of the survivors in Plimoth begin to turn. Friendly Indians help your settlement and in the autumn the colonists and their Indian allies enjoy the first Thanksgiving meal on American soil.

Squanto

DURING MARCH the Pilgrims are visited by Squanto, a Pawtuxet Indian who speaks some English.

SQUANTO explains how he came to learn the language. He had been captured by the English in 1614.

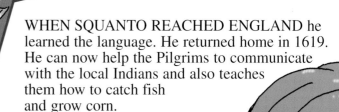

WHEN SQUANTO REACHED ENGLAND he learned the language. He returned home in 1619. He can now help the Pilgrims to communicate with the local Indians and also teaches them how to catch fish and grow corn.

The Mayflower Legacy

*I*n the years that follow, the colony grows and new settlements are established. You marry John Alden, the cooper from the *Mayflower*, and raise nine children. Today, your legacy and that of the other passengers aboard the *Mayflower*, has spread throughout the United States. It is estimated that 35 million Americans — 12% of the total population — are direct descendants of the first Mayflower Pilgrims. You may have risked everything during that dangerous voyage to a new land, but your descendants now enjoy the freedom that the Pilgrims were seeking when they first set sail: beginning a voyage that, in the end, you are glad you made.

Your Descendants

YOUR FAMILY'S descendants include many famous Americans.

JOHN ADAMS (1735-1826). Became the second president of the United States in 1797.

JOHN QUINCY ADAMS (1767-1848). The son of John, became the sixth president.

Handy Hint

Try to survive and raise lots of children — your ancestors will be grateful!

A THRIVING COMMUNITY. The Plimoth colony grew and prospered over the years. Today, the town of Plymouth is a popular tourist attraction. A replica of the *Mayflower* in the harbor and a reconstruction of the Plimoth Plantation attract visitors from around the world.

HENRY WADSWORTH LONGFELLOW (1807-1882). A popular and influential poet.

WILLIAM CULLEN BRYANT (1794-1878). A journalist, critic and poet.

ORSON WELLES (1915-1985), actor-director and MARILYN MONROE (1926-1962), actress.

29

Glossary

Bowsprit A small mast that projects from the front of a ship.

Civil rights Personal and property rights that are legal and recognized by the government.

Colony A distant territory settled by emigrants, which is under the control of their home country.

Congregation A group of people who gather together for religious worship.

Contingent A group of people who represent an area or a larger group.

Cooper A craftsman who makes and repairs wooden barrels.

Democracy A government elected by the people.

Descendant A person whose history can be traced to a particular individual or family.

Emigrate To leave one country to settle in another.

Flintlock musket An early form of a gun.

Landfall The land that is sighted or reached after a voyage.

Legacy Something that is handed down from an ancestor from the past.

New World A term used to describe America.

Oakum Hemp or jute fiber, usually mixed with tar, that was used for to make wooden ships watertight.

Pilgrims The name first used by William Bradford to describe the group of Separatists that moved to Leiden. The term Pilgrims was used later to describe all of the Separatists that traveled to America aboard the Mayflower.

Plimoth Colony The settlement established by the Pilgrims at present-day Plymouth, Massachusetts in December 1620. The Pilgrims misspelled the name in their original documents.

Poop house The living quarters of the captain on board ship, located at the stern and above the level of the main deck.

Puritans The name given in the 16th century to the more extreme English Protestants who believed in strict religious discipline.

Seaworthy A ship or boat that is capable of sailing on open seas without undue risk of sinking.

Separatists Radical Puritans who broke away from the Church of England during the reign of Queen Elizabeth I to establish their own independent congregations.

Shallop A small open boat, used primarily in shallow water.

Treaty A formal agreement between two or more groups to establish terms of peace or trade.

Whip-staff A vertical wooden bar attached to a tiller, which in turn was attached to the rudder, to steer a ship.

Index

White Eagle LMC
1585 White Eagle Drive
Naperville, IL 60564